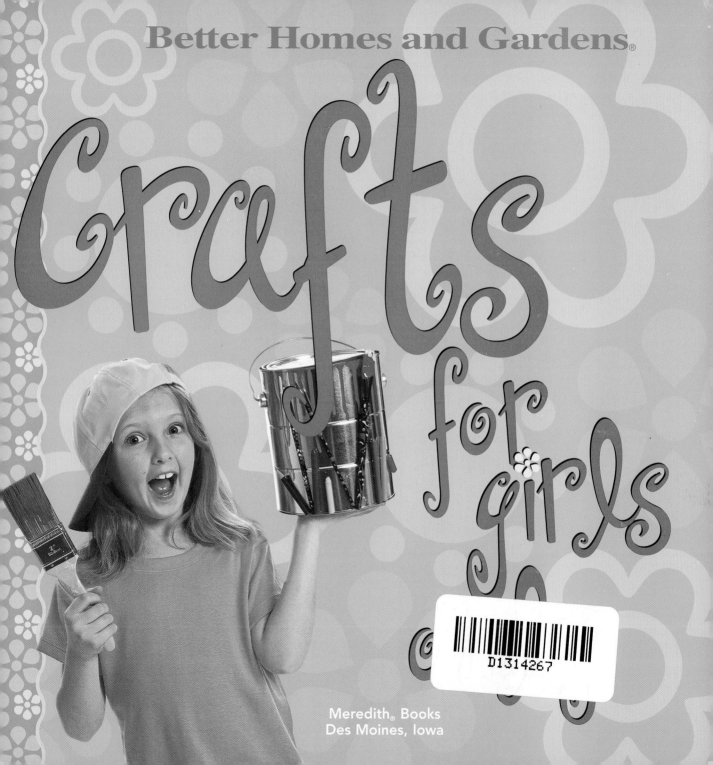

Better Homes and Gardens®

Crafts
for girls

Meredith® Books
Des Moines, Iowa

D1314267

Crafts for girls only

Editor: Carol Field Dahlstrom
Writer: Susan M. Banker
Designer: Angie Haupert Hoogensen
Copy Chief: Terri Fredrickson
Copy and Production Editor: Victoria Forlini
Editorial Operations Manager: Karen Schirm
Managers, Book Production: Pam Kvitne, Marjorie J. Schenkelberg, Rick von Holdt
Contributing Copy Editor: Arianna McKinney
Contributing Proofreaders: Beth Havey, Colleen Johnson, Anne E. Terpstra
Photographers: Scott Little, Andy Lyons Cameraworks, Jay Wilde
Technical Illustrator: Shawn Drafahl
Technical Assistant: Judy Bailey
Editorial and Design Assistants: Kaye Chabot, Mary Lee Gavin, Karen McFadden

Meredith® Books
Editor in Chief: Linda Raglan Cunningham
Design Director: Matt Strelecki
Executive Editor, Food and Crafts: Jennifer Dorland Darling

Publisher: James D. Blume
Executive Director, Marketing: Jeffrey Myers
Executive Director, New Business Development: Todd M. Davis
Executive Director, Sales: Ken Zagor
Director, Operations: George A. Susral
Director, Production: Douglas M. Johnston
Business Director: Jim Leonard

Vice President and General Manager: Douglas J. Guendel

Better Homes and Gardens® Magazine
Editor in Chief: Karol DeWulf Nickell

Meredith Publishing Group
President, Publishing Group: Stephen M. Lacy
Vice President-Publishing Director: Bob Mate

Meredith Corporation
Chairman and Chief Executive Officer: William T. Kerr

In Memoriam: E. T. Meredith III (1933-2003)

All of us at Better Homes and Gardens® Books are dedicated to providing you with information and ideas to create beautiful and useful projects. We welcome your comments and suggestions. Write to us at: Meredith Books, Crafts Editorial Department, 1716 Locust Street—LN112, Des Moines, IA 50309-3023.

If you would like to purchase any of our crafts, cooking, gardening, home improvement, or home decorating and design books, check wherever quality books are sold. Or visit us at: bhgbooks.com

Cover Photograph: Andy Lyons Cameraworks

Girls Just Gotta Have Fun!

Okay, girls! It's time to have fun—and nothing is more fun than crafting! We know how much you like to make things and how talented you are! So in this book we've shared some great crafts you can make to show off your awesome talents! You'll find phones to paint, lampshades to laugh at, crazy-looking clocks, pretty piggy banks, jazzy jewelry, and some snazzy shoes. You'll find ideas for your room, gifts you can make for your friends and family, things you'll love to make and wear, and far-out crafting ideas to bring out the artist in you. You'll get to paint, bead, sew, work with clay, color with markers, and design with felt and leather. So grab your crafting supplies (and maybe your best girlfriend) and start crafting...because girls just gotta have fun!

Carol Field Dahlstrom

Contents

1

GO TO YOUR ROOM— AND LOVE IT!

Awesome Ideas to Make Your Room Rock

2

FROM YOURS TRULY!

Great Gifts to Make for Your Friends and Family

3

LOOK AT YOU!

You'll Be Stylin' with Great Things to Make and Wear

PAGES 66-91

4

GO AHEAD— GET ARTSY!

No Special Reason, Just Craft for the Fun of It

PAGES 92-123

Hey Girls!

Crafting is such a blast! There are tons of cool supplies out there to help you make just about anything you could ever want!

This book shows you dozens of great crafts for girls—like accessories that will make your room even more fun to come home to and things to wear that everyone in your class will envy.

Plus, find wonderful gift ideas for your family and friends —awesome presents they will love to receive.

You may already know some of the ways to make the projects, but look for brand new ideas as well. To get you started, a complete list of supplies you need is with every project. Some things on the list are already around the house, but others will probably mean shopping with Mom at your local crafts store which is always way fun! If you are unsure of what a supply or technique is, check the glossary on pages 124–125 for help.

Look for the "Amazing" symbol above (as well as "It's Easy") to give you even more crafting ideas and tips. Become a pro in a flash!

After gathering the needed supplies, follow the instructions step by step to make a project like the one in the photo. The instructions and how-to photos help you through some of the more unusual steps. If there are techniques or supplies which need an adult's help, you'll see that in the instructions as well.

Sprinkled throughout the book are tips and ideas to stretch your imagination. These pointers will help you make your own original, fantastic crafts—so have fun experimenting with supplies and using the techniques you learn— just go for it!

Once you are familiar with different crafting supplies and what to do with them, you'll want to teach your friends how to craft something totally cool. Just being together, making things, and sharing supplies is half the fun of crafting. And what could be better than having this book to go by? It's jammed full of ideas FOR GIRLS ONLY!

GO TO YOUR ROOM— AND LOVE IT!

Awesome Ideas to Make Your Room Rock

Hang out in your room with totally cool stuff you make yourself—a hand-painted phone, trendy organizers, and signs that rule!

Ladylike Lamp

what you'll need

Tracing paper; pencil
Fine-line permanent
    marking pen

Smooth white
    lampshade, about
    4-inches in diameter
    at the top and
    9-inches at the bottom
Silver dress maker's
    pencil (available at
    fabric stores)
Colored pencils
    (soft lead)

Powdered pink blush
    and purple eye
    shadow
Cotton swab
Acrylic paint in red
    and white
Paintbrush
Nonscented hair spray
Thick white crafts glue
Dark color oval gem for
    eye pupil
18 inches of fringe in
    yellow or other color
10 inches of ribbon for
    hair bow

here's how

Trace the face pattern
you like, *pages 12–13*,
on tracing paper and
outline the features with
a marking pen. Put the
paper on the inside of
shade in center front. You
should be able to see the
pattern through the

shade. Use the silver dressmaker's pencil to outline the features on the shade front.

2 Use colored pencils to color in the eyes and eyebrows. Outline all pattern lines with the marking pen.

3 Apply eye shadow above eye with a cotton swab.

4 Use your finger or brush to put blush on the cheek areas.

5 Thin red paint with water and paint the lips. Use white acrylic paint to make a white highlight in the eye. Let dry.

6 Spray the lampshade with a light coat of hair spray to seal.

7 Glue the gem in the center of the eye.

8 Glue the fringe around the top of the shade. Glue center strands to side to form a part.

9 Tie ribbon in a bow and glue to rim.

Give a lampshade personality that will lighten up any room.

Ladylike Lamp

LAMP FACE PATTERN

ALTERNATE LAMP FACE PATTERN

13

Pretty-up recycled
bottles to show off
in your room!

14

Dressed-Up Bottles

what You'll need for the short bottle

Plain glass bottle with cork
White glass paint, such as
   Liquitex Glossies
Thick white crafts glue
Paintbrush; ⅛-inch-wide
   blue satin ribbon
12 white shirt buttons
Large button

what You'll need for the tall bottle

Plain glass bottle; glass
   paints, such as Liquitex
   Glossies, in cream and
   bright blue; paintbrush
Colored pencils (soft lead)
Newspapers
Clear acrylic spray

here's how

1 For the short bottle, paint the top half of the bottle white, making a V on each side. Let the paint dry. Have an adult help you bake the bottle in the oven as directed by the paint manufacturer. Let cool. Glue three up and down strips of ribbon on each side of the bottle. Glue strips of ribbon along the edges of the painted areas. Glue another strip of ribbon around the neck of bottle. Glue three shirt buttons over the center ribbon on each side. Glue a ribbon to make an X across the top of the cork. Glue a large button to the top of the cork.

2 For the tall bottle, paint the bottom two-thirds with cream and the top one-third with bright blue. Let dry. Apply a second coat if needed; let dry. Have an adult help you bake the bottle in the oven as directed by the paint manufacturer. Let cool. Use colored pencils to draw simple flowers, stems, and leaves on the sides. Have an adult help you place the bottle on the newspapers and spray with a light coat of clear acrylic.

IT'S EASY!

Decorate nifty bottles for only pennies. Find other fantastic trims to dress them up, such as:
* Stickers
* Silk flowers and leaves
* Postage stamps
* Small plastic toys

what You'll need

Old dark and light denim
   jeans; scissors; ruler
Six 4-inch cork squares
Hot-glue gun; glue sticks
Brad paper fastener
8×12-inch piece of stiff
   felt sheet
½-inch-wide yellow
   ribbon; baby rickrack
Wire cutters; silk flowers
Plastic thumbtacks
Strong glue, such as
   Aleene's Platinum Bond

here's how

1 From each color of denim, cut three 5-inch squares.

2 Place each cork square in the center of a denim square. With adult help, place hot-glue along one edge of the cork and wrap the denim edges around the cork. Repeat on the opposite edge of the cork and again on the two remaining sides as shown in Photo A, stretching the fabric tightly each time.

3 Carefully poke the brad fastener through the center of the felt sheet 1½ inches down from the top edge. To make a hanger for the bulletin board, tie a loop of ribbon around the brad ends. Separate the metal ends flat against the felt. Glue the wrong side of each cork square to the felt as shown in Photo B.

4 Hot-glue rickrack around board edges.

5 To make floral tacks, use wire cutters to trim flower heads off stems. Use strong glue to attach a flower to each thumbtack head. Let dry.

Blooming Bulletin Board

Keep all your notes handy with a denim bulletin board and fancy floral thumbtacks.

Create a wall clock that makes you smile whenever you check the time.

Crazy Clock

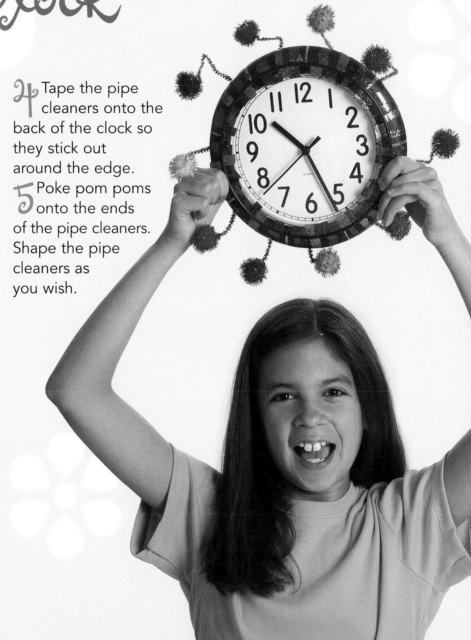

what You'll need
**Adhesive metallic papers
(available at
scrapbooking stores)
Scissors; round wall clock
with wide frame
Colored pipe cleaners
Tape; pom-poms**

here's how
1 Cut pieces of metallic
papers in different shapes
small enough to fit in the
inner rim of the clock. Stick
them on without leaving
space between the shapes.

2 Cut metallic papers in
larger shapes long
enough to cover the outside
rim of the clock. Place the
papers on the rim, spacing
them about ½ inch apart.

3 Stick the leftover papers
wherever you want on
the clock rim.

4 Tape the pipe
cleaners onto the
back of the clock so
they stick out
around the edge.

5 Poke pom poms
onto the ends
of the pipe cleaners.
Shape the pipe
cleaners as
you wish.

Fancy Floral Phone

what You'll need

- **Soft damp rag**
- **Black purse-style phone (available at department stores)**
- **Acrylic enamel paints in bright pink, yellow, green, red, purple, orange, and white**
- **Small round paintbrush**
- **Thick white crafts glue**
- **Toothpick; round acrylic gems in paint colors and turquoise**

here's how

1 Wipe the phone off with a damp rag and let it dry. Avoid touching the areas to be painted.

2 Remove the hand piece from the phone base while you paint. To paint flowers, start with the round centers. Paint dime- to nickel-size circles in several colors, leaving space for petals, leaves, and spirals. Paint a circle in the center of the dial, as shown in Photo A (page 22). Let the paint dry.

3 To make petals for each flower, get a little paint on a small round brush. Using the side of the bristles, place

continued on page 22

Chitchatting with girlfriends is more fun than ever with bright sparkling flowers blooming on your phone.

Fancy Floral Phone

continued from page 20

the point of the brush next to the circular flower center and press down as shown in Photo B. Continue spacing petals of the same color evenly around the center. Make petals for each flower. Let dry.

4 Paint green leaves and thin spirals between the flowers, using Photo C as a guide. To fill in blank areas with white dots, dip the paintbrush handle in paint and dot on the surface in groups of three. Let the paint dry.

5 Use a toothpick to dot glue where you wish to put gems,

working with only a few dots at a time. To pick up and place tiny gems, use a toothpick with just enough glue on it to be tacky. Using fingers, press larger gems into the glue on the phone as shown in Photo D. Continue adding gems until all flower centers, leaf veins, and spirals are decorated. Let the glue dry.

Rainbow Room Accessories

Brighten your favorite hangout with a burst of color by wrapping a tissue box and trash can with textured yarn.

what You'll need

Plain tissue box cover and wastepaper basket
Felt
Marking pen; scissors
Thick white crafts glue
Crafts stick; colorful textured yarn

continued on page 26

IT'S EASY!

This project is so easy to do, you can make it while watching your favorite TV show! Just be sure to work on newspapers so Mom doesn't have to worry about glue drips!

Rainbow Room Accessories

continued from page 23

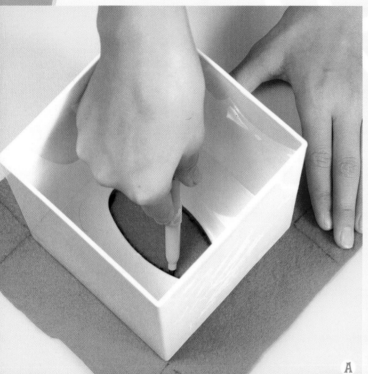

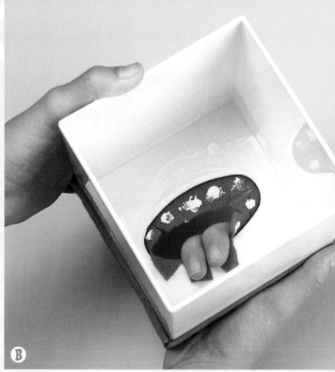

Ⓐ Ⓑ

here's how

1 Turn the tissue box cover upside down on felt. About 1½ inches from the felt edge, draw a line around the outer edge of the tissue box with marking pen. Cut out.

Place cover in the center of the cut-out felt and draw squares from each corner. Trace the opening in the top as shown in Photo A. For the opening, cut slits from the center to the outline. Cut away the corner squares.

2 Use a crafts stick to spread white glue on top of tissue box cover and 1 inch down the sides. Place the piece of felt over the top,

smoothing it along the top and down the sides. Spread a small amount of glue on the inside around the opening and fold the clipped felt into the inside of the box as shown in Photo B, *opposite*.

3 Spread glue around the sides of the tissue box, working from top to bottom. Wind yarn around box, spreading more glue as needed.

4 To cover the wastepaper basket, spread glue around the top edge and wrap the basket with yarn. Repeat around sides until the entire basket is covered with yarn, spreading more glue as you work. Let the glue dry.

AMAZING!

Wrap your accessories with other materials too! Try using raffia, string, jute, embroidery floss, beads on a string, or even narrow strips of torn fabric to wrap your room accessories with color and texture!

27

Girls Only Sign

Beware boys–this room is for girlfriends!

what You'll need

Decorative-edge scissors
Crafting foam: 2 sheets
   black, plus 1 sheet
   each of purple, green,
   yellow, pink, and a
   patterned sheet or
   4 desired colors
Letter stamps
White acrylic paint
Scissors
Permanent black
   marking pen
Thick white crafts glue
Wide ribbon
Tape

here's how

1. Use decorative-edge scissors to trim off the edge of the patterned sheet of foam.

2. Glue the patterned piece onto a full sheet of black so the black edge shows.

3. Choose the colors of foam you wish to use for the letters and decide what order you want them in. Stamp the letter by placing the stamp in white paint and stamping onto the foam surface as shown in Photo A. Let dry.

4. Cut out rectangles around letters as shown in Photo B.

5. Outline the letters with black marking pen.

6. Use decorative-edge scissors to cut out different colors of foam to back the letters, making shapes slightly larger than the letter rectangles.

7. Glue the letters onto the backing cut shapes.

8. Lay the letters on the work surface to see how much space is needed to spell the words. Cut a rectangle from black foam to back the letters. Cut a decorative-edge rectangle from yellow foam slightly smaller than the black. Glue the yellow to the black so the edge shows.

9. Arrange and overlap the letters on the yellow foam. Glue the letters in place. Tie the ribbon in a bow. Glue the ends to the sign back.

A

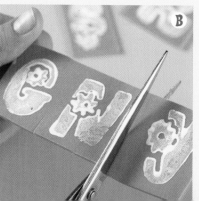
B

what you'll need

Ceramic piggy bank, available at crafts and discount stores
Acrylic paints in colors you like
Paintbrush
Glitter and plain paint in tubes
Strong glue, such as E6000
Gems, buttons, and jewelry pieces
Feathers

here's how

1 Begin with a clean dry piggy bank. Paint the bank one solid color or paint sections different colors. Let the paint dry.

2 Draw designs on the bank using a tube of glitter paint. Let dry.

3 Ask an adult to help you glue trims where you like. Let the glue dry.

Penny the Piggy Bank

AMAZING!

Banks come in all shapes and sizes. Choose a bank you like and decorate it with old jewelry, pictures from greeting cards, and other silly stuff! (For fun, have your friends write secrets you share on small pieces of paper and keep them hidden in a bank with an opening in the bottom. When you get together again, sprinkle out the papers and have fun giggling at what you wrote!)

Dress up your piggy bank with fancy and funky fashion using bright and sparkly trims.

Beautiful Room Organizers

Butterfly

Please you and Mom too! Keep your room super neat with fun organizers you decorate yourself.

what You'll need

Oven-bake clay, such as Premo, in colors you like
Rolling pin; scissors
1½-inch-long jewelry wires
Flat bottom glass baking dish
Glue; metal trash can, box, and pencil holder
Permanent black marking pen

continued on page 34

continued from page 32

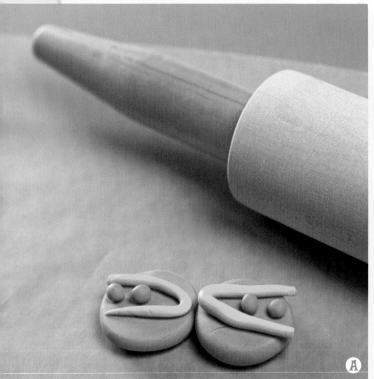

Ⓐ Ⓑ

here's how

1 For each pair of wings, use a rolling pin to flatten two large grape-size ovals until about ¼ inch thick. To create designs, use different clay colors to make small coils, ropes, or balls. Place shapes on flattened clay, making similar designs on a pair of pieces as shown in Photo A. Place waxed paper over clay and flatten with a rolling pin.

2 For each butterfly body, make four or five clay ropes, each about 8 inches long. Twist the ropes together as shown in Photo B. Fold the clay coil in half and twist again, making a rounded head and a narrow tail as shown in Photo C. For antennae,

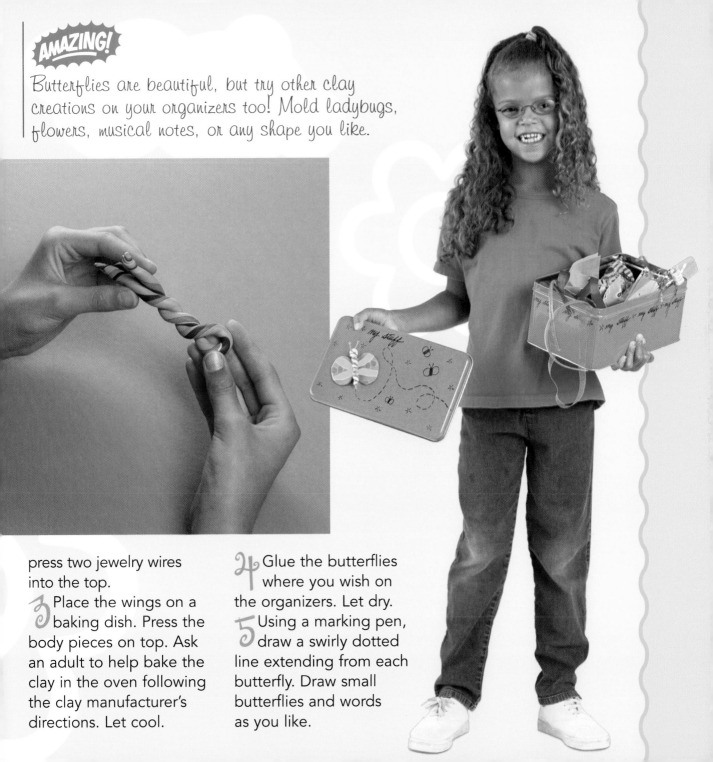

Butterflies are beautiful, but try other clay creations on your organizers too! Mold ladybugs, flowers, musical notes, or any shape you like.

press two jewelry wires into the top.

3 Place the wings on a baking dish. Press the body pieces on top. Ask an adult to help bake the clay in the oven following the clay manufacturer's directions. Let cool.

4 Glue the butterflies where you wish on the organizers. Let dry.

5 Using a marking pen, draw a swirly dotted line extending from each butterfly. Draw small butterflies and words as you like.

School

Shopping

Time

A Movie

Slumber Party

For

Dance

Beauty Regime

Pastime Sign

Let everyone know what you enjoy most with this clever sign in the shape of a clock.

IT'S EASY!

Personalize the frame of a real wall clock with all your favorite pastimes too! Just glue the stickered foam circles all around the frame of the real clock.

what You'll need

Pencil
Foam board or cardboard from frozen pizza package
Crafts knife
Crafting foam in yellow, pink, purple, and striped
Scissors
Double-sided tape
Decorative-edge scissors, if desired
Flower brads
Black adhesive lettering in ½- and 1-inch sizes
Grosgrain ribbon
Stapler

here's how

1 If using a foam board, draw a 12-inch-wide circle on board. Ask an adult to cut out the circle using a crafts knife.

2 Lay the circle on yellow foam and trace with a pencil. Cut out the yellow circle with scissors and apply to the foam board with double-sided tape. Using the pattern on *page 39*, cut out six squares from striped foam, three circles from pink, and three circles from purple. Cut out the arrow from purple foam.

continued on page 38

Pastime Sign

continued from page 37

3 Use double-sided tape to stick foam circles to foam squares. Stick foam squares onto the large yellow foam circle. Press the foam arrow pieces together using double-sided tape.

4 Ask an adult to insert the crafts knife into each circle-square to make a small slit for a flower brad. Insert the brads. Ask an adult to make a slit in the arrow arm and in the center of the foam board base. Insert the brad through arrow and base.

5 Using the photo on *page 36* as a guide, press adhesive letters on the face of the clock. Staple grosgrain ribbon on the clock back for hanging.

AMAZING!

When you start to think about what to put on your Pastime Sign, you might be surprised at all the things you like to do! Here are some ideas to get you started...

* Hug mom and dad
* Hug my sister
* Hug my brother
* Play soccer
* Practice piano
* Girl chat
* Make popcorn
* Have snack time
* Play with the dog
* Play with the cat
* Take a nap
* Read
* Ride bike
* Take a walk
* Eat pizza
* Sing, sing, sing

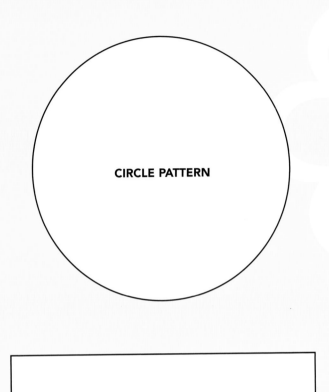

CIRCLE PATTERN

SQUARE PATTERN

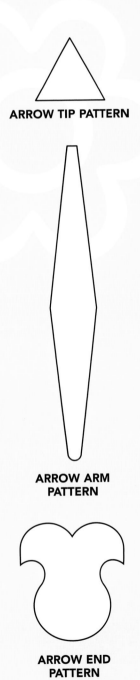

ARROW TIP PATTERN

**ARROW ARM
PATTERN**

**ARROW END
PATTERN**

Have you seen the news?

2

FROM YOURS TRULY!

Great Gifts to Make for Your Friends and Family

Show your mom and dad (and your friends too!) how artistic and crafty you are by making gifts just for them.

Make your best pal a simply divine journal to record all her deepest thoughts.

Best Friend Journal

what you'll need

Journal
Acrylic paint in friend's
  favorite color
Paintbrush
Decoupage medium
Fibers, such as string,
  knotty yarn, or
  embroidery floss
Scissors; flat decorative
  trim or shank button
  (the kind with a loop
  on back); wire cutters
Thick white crafts glue

here's how

1 Paint the journal with acrylic paint. Let it dry.

2 Paint over the front of cover with decoupage medium. While wet, wrap the fibers around the cover as desired. Brush over the fibers and entire cover with more decoupage medium. Let dry.

3 Have an adult help you clip off the shank of the button using wire cutters.

4 Glue the button in place. Let dry.

43

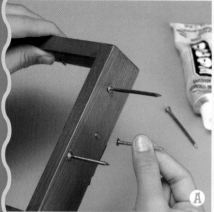

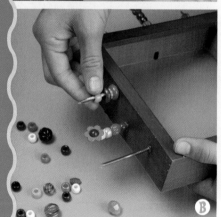

Instead of using real beads you could make them by painting pasta (any kind with holes!) with acrylic paint. These handmade creations work great for this project!

what You'll need

Long nails that fit through beads
Beads and buttons with wide holes
Acrylic paint in any color you wish
Paintbrush
Strong glue, such as E6000
Wide shadow box-style frame
Thick white crafts glue

here's how

1 Choose nails and beads, making sure the beads fit on the nails. Paint the heads of the nails with acrylic paint. Let dry.

2 Use a small dab of strong glue to attach the nails onto one side of the frame as shown in Photo A. Let dry. Glue nails on two more sides. Let dry.

3 Starting at the bottom of the nail, dab a small dot of crafts glue onto the nail, place a few beads on the nail, dab more glue, and then place more beads to cover the nail as shown in Photo B. Place a button on the end of the nail if you wish.

Funky Frame

Make a super cool gift by trimming a frame
with easy-to-do beaded rays!

Treasure Boxes

what you'll need

Heart-shape cardboard boxes with lids
Acrylic paint in colors you like
Paintbrush
Glitter in colors you like
White texturizing medium and texturizing tips, such as Susan Scheewe (available with the paints in the fine art section of crafts stores)
Table knife

These adorable boxes prove that good things come in small packages.

here's how

1 Paint the bottom half of the box. Sprinkle a little glitter on the wet paint. Let the paint dry.

2 Decorate the lids with the white texturizing medium just like decorating cookies. Spread it on thick and smooth with a knife, making swirls or other simple designs. Use a texturizing tip to draw lines or other details. Use the flower shape tip to create the look of spiked frosting (like on the green box lid, *opposite*).

3 While the texturizing medium is wet, sprinkle with glitter. Let the texturizing medium dry before touching it.

IT'S EASY!

Since these heart boxes are so much fun to make, design one for each of your friends. Make several in different colors and give them away when it's a friend's birthday or when someone special needs a hug.

Cheery Checkbook Covers

what You'll need

Clear checkbook cover, available at crafts stores

Assorted colored papers

Decorative-edge scissors

Scissors

Thick white crafts glue

Flat decorations, such as sequins, silk flowers, fibers, or feathers

Adhesive lettering

here's how

1 Carefully remove the paper insert from inside the checkbook cover.

2 Cut or tear papers to cover the paper insert. Layer and glue the papers on the insert. Trim off the extra paper at the edges.

3 Use glue to attach sequins, silk flowers, fibers, or feathers on paper insert.

4 Use adhesive letters to spell a name or whatever words you wish.

Watch your favorite grown-ups smile when you present their very own artistic checkbook covers made by you!

49

PRETTY BOW TOPPER

BUTTERFLY TOPPER

Pretty Pencils

Friends will have even more fun doodling when you give them pencils wrapped in colorful floss and topped with ribbon!

what You'll need
Scissors
Attachable eraser cap
   for pencil
Thick white crafts glue
Embroidery floss in
   desired colors
Mechanical pencil
1½- and 3-inch-wide
   wire-edge ribbons
Pipe cleaners; beads
Tacks

here's how

1 For either pencil, trim off the tip of the eraser cap using scissors to make it flat. Place it on end of mechanical pencil.

2 Dab glue on the eraser and wrap embroidery floss around eraser as shown in Photo A. Continue to wrap down the mechanical pencil, applying glue as needed. Avoid wrapping the pencil where it clicks to push out the lead.

3 *To make a Bow Topper, opposite top,* cut a piece of ribbon about 20 inches long. Hold the ribbon in the center and loop the ends back and forth, making 4-inch-long loops. Tie in the center with floss. To trim the ribbon ends in Vs, fold each piece in half lengthwise and make a diagonal cut from the fold upward.

4 *To make a Butterfly Topper, opposite bottom,* cut a 5-inch piece of the wide ribbon. Fold the ribbon in half and make V cuts on either end. Unfold. Cut a 3½-inch piece from narrower ribbon. Layer the two; set aside. Cut a 6-inch piece of pipe cleaner. Place a bead on each end and bend to hold bead in place. Fold the pipe cleaner into a V and place it around the ribbons as shown in Photo B. Twist to secure.

5 Press a tack through the ribbon design and insert it into the pencil top as shown in Photo C.

IT'S EASY!

Give other plain handles a hue too. Use embroidery floss to wrap the handles of hairbrushes, mirrors, and paintbrushes.

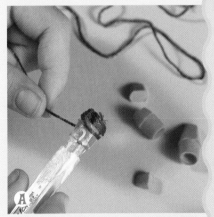

TV tidbits

what You'll need

5½×8½-inch piece of
 colored paper; scissors
Colored card stock
Glue stick; orange/yellow
 and silver holographic
 sticker sheets
Papers in blue and white
⅛-inch paper punch
Tape; black marking pen

here's how

1 Fold colored paper in half in both directions; crease. Unfold, showing an X in the center.

2 To cut pop-up, refold paper lengthwise. Cut pop-up below center crease; when completed the top half of the paper folds down making the card back and covers the cut opening, see photo, *opposite*. Cutting downward, make two 1-inch-long cuts through both layers of folded paper 2¼ inches apart (one cut is 1 inch from side edge and one is 1 inch down from the middle crease); unfold. Lengthen the end of the cuts on one side of the card by ½ inch.

3 Refold the card in half widthwise. Pull up on paper between cuts and crease the loop center. Decorate pop-up and card front using patterns, *right,* to cut papers and sticker sheets.

ANTENNA PATTERN

CARD FRONT
TV SCREEN
PATTERN

CARD FRONT
TV PATTERN

POP-UP TV SCREEN
PATTERN

FOLD

POP-UP TV PATTERN

Make a cool pop-up card to share with a friend who loves to watch TV.

In-the-Bag Note Cards

what You'll need

Tracing paper
Pencil
Scissors
Heavyweight solid and
   patterned scrapbook
   papers
Mini brad paper
   fasteners
Colored vellum
Glue stick
¾- and ⅝-inch paper
   punches
Adhesive hook-and-loop
   tape, such as Velcro
Envelope

here's how

1 Trace the patterns, *page 57*; cut out the shapes.

2 Fold both the patterned paper and the vellum in half. Place the purse pattern against the fold line and trace the shape onto each piece. Cut out the purse shape from both papers. Use the handle pattern to cut two shapes from solid paper.

continued on page 56

Fun scrapbook papers cut in mini purse shapes send fashionable statements. The handles, attached with brad paper fasteners, make these cute cards look like real totes.

In-the-Bag Note Cards

continued from page 55

3 Open the patterned paper purse and place the handle ends at the top of the purse on the outside. Ask an adult to help you cut slits through the handle ends and purse top (as shown by the dots on the purse handle pattern). Thread mini brads through the slits; separate the metal ends on the inside of the card.

4 Cut the closure strip from solid paper using the pattern, *opposite*. Fold it on the line shown. Glue one end to the inside back of the patterned purse. Glue two punched or hand-cut circles (using patterns) to the other end of the paper strip. Press one side of the adhesive tape under the circle and the other side to the front of the purse. Glue the vellum purse inside the finished patterned paper purse. Glue another color of paper inside the card if you wish.

AMAZING!

Use this paper purse for a really terrific birthday card. On the inside write "Hope your day holds all good things for you!"

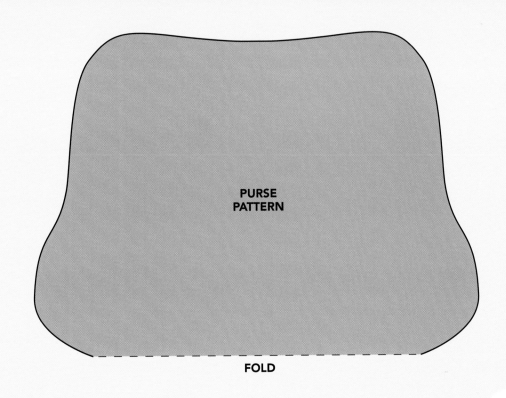

PURSE PATTERN

FOLD

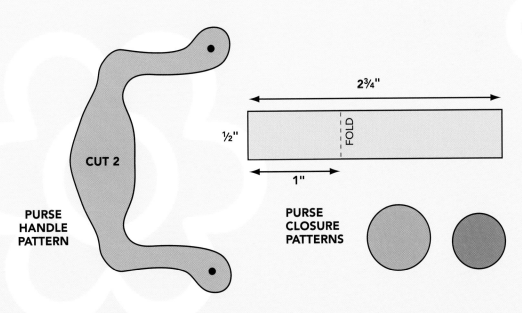

CUT 2

PURSE HANDLE PATTERN

2¾"

½"

FOLD

1"

PURSE CLOSURE PATTERNS

what you'll need

**Paper in colors and
  patterns you like**
Scissors
**Decorative-edge
  scissors, optional**
**Sequins, round and
  shapes**
Toothpick
Thick white crafts glue
String
Fine-line marking pen
Pencil; jar lid

Make all sorts of cards and gift tags by recycling old greeting cards, envelopes, and grocery bags! Add sequin designs to make extra special greetings.

Make your thank you sparkle with sequins in your favorite colors!

here's how

1 Fold a piece of paper in half. Cut the card any size you like. Use decorative-edge scissors to trim one edge if you wish. Layer a smaller piece of paper on the top for a two-tone card.

2 Using the cards, *opposite*, for ideas, decide on a design. Use a toothpick to glue the sequins in place on the card front.

3 For the sequin flower trio card, glue string in place. For the single flower card, glue a paper strip stem in the center.

4 Use a marking pen to write words on the card. Hint: Trace a jar lid with a pencil to write the words in a circular shape. Erase the pencil lines when you are done.

A great Big Thanks!

Pamper a pal by making her a pretty jar filled with relaxing bath salts.

Tub-Time Treat

what you'll need

Large and small mixing
bowls
3 cups Epsom salts
1 cup baking soda
A few drops of
lavender oil
Water
Food coloring
Tablespoon
Large spoon
Shallow dish
Glass canister or jar
with lid
Thick white crafts glue
Shells
Glitter
Small seed beads
Coordinating ribbon

here's how

1 In a large bowl, mix the Epsom salts, baking soda, and lavender oil. Place a tablespoon of water in a small bowl and mix in as much food coloring as you wish; add to the salt and soda mixture. Stir until thoroughly colored and blended as shown in Photo A.

2 Spread out the mixture on a shallow dish. Stir it every now and then with a spoon to help it dry as shown in Photo B.

3 Coat the jar lid with a large amount of glue. Place shells in glue and then sprinkle with glitter and small beads. Let dry.

4 Fill the jar with the bath salts and tie a ribbon around the top.

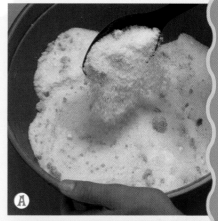

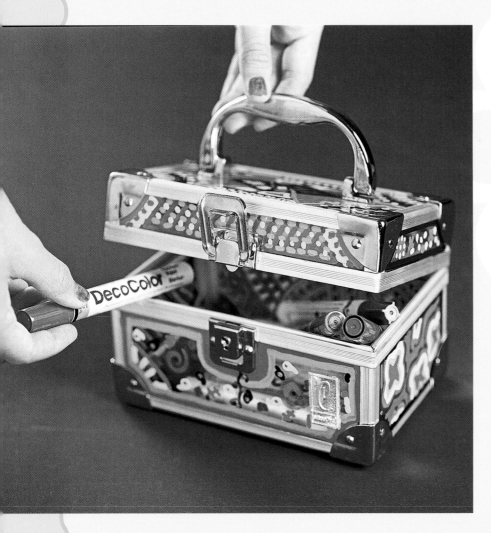

Art Case

what you'll need
**Clear acrylic box
(available in drug and
discount stores by the
cosmetics)
Paint pens in a variety
of colors**

here's how
1 Cover the flat
background areas of
the case with paint pens,
drawing whatever
patterns and shapes
you like.

2 To make a floral
design, such as the
one shown on the side of
the case, draw a small
flower shape, then
outline it again and again
in several colors. Let dry.

AMAZING!
Decorate a whole suitcase using paint
pens. Hard-surfaced cases are easiest to
write on, but soft vinyl cases work too!

Fashion a case with all your
favorite colors and designs to give
to your best buddy.

Cover a metal container with clay for a cleverly disguised bedroom organizer.

Bold Brush Bin

what You'll need

Polymer clay, such as Sculpey
Rolling pin
Decorative-edge scissors
Glaze/adhesive, such as Liquid Sculpey
Metal container
Screwdriver, ball point pen, buttons, or other items to make marks in clay

here's how

1 Knead the clay until it is soft and very workable. For the background, roll out several colors on a smooth surface to about 1/8 inch thick.

2 Cut the flattened clay pieces into irregular shapes with decorative-edge scissors as shown in Photo A,

right. Spread a small amount of glaze/adhesive onto the surface. Press the shapes onto side of container as shown in Photo B.

3 Layer on clay details, such as shapes, dots, and squiggles. For dots, roll small amounts of clay into balls and press onto surface. Top this with a smaller ball of clay in a different color.

4 For texture, use a screwdriver, pen with the tip retracted, buttons, or other items to make marks in the clay.

5 Roll two different colors of clay, such as black and white, into long ropes. Twist the ropes together to make a trim for the top edge of the container.

A

B

6 Ask an adult to help you bake the container in the oven according to the directions on the clay label.

3

LOOK AT YOU!

You'll be Stylin' with Great Things to Make and Wear

Get ready to have a hip new look with original purses, hair bands, and jewelry that you fashion.

Recycle worn-out jeans by making a cute-as-a-button purse for each of your friends.

Pocket Purses

what you'll need

Scissors
Old jeans
Fabric glue, such as
    Beacon's FabricTac
Patterned fabric scraps
Decoupage medium
Paintbrush
Beaded trim or fringe
Buttons
¼-inch black elastic
Sewing needle
Black thread
Seam sealant

here's how

1 Cut around a back pocket from jeans, leaving seams intact to prevent unraveling. Leave an inch or two of fabric above the pocket to make a flap if you wish.

continued on page 70

Pocket Purses

continued from page 69

To make a purse that also has a cell phone pocket, cut around a narrow pocket from carpenter's pants and glue it to the wrong side of the back pocket.

2 Cut the length of the side seams out of the pant leg and set it aside for the purse strap. Use fabric glue to glue beaded trim or fringe to both the top flap and bottom edge of pocket.

3 Cut out a design from a fabric scrap. Brush decoupage medium on the back of the cutout, put it on the front of the pocket, and brush over the surface with more decoupage medium. Let dry.

4 Make a loop out of a 3-inch length of elastic; knot the ends. With a needle and thread, stitch the knot to the center underside of flap edge.

5 Look at the photos, *opposite*, to learn how to stitch a button to the center front of the purse. Place it so the elastic loop can hook over it. (The denim strip in the photo is for demonstration only. It is not part of project.)

6 Stitch the ends of side seam strap into the top of either side of the pocket. Apply seam sealant to the cut edges.

Use your imagination to find other materials for a purse handle. Consider stitching chains, old belts, ribbon, shoelaces, and braided trims to the sides of the purse.

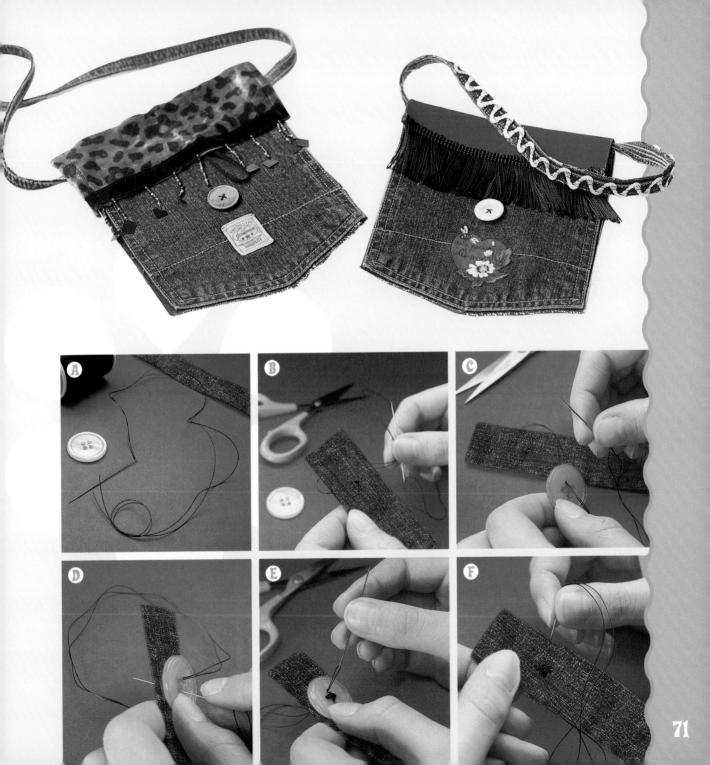

what You'll need

Suede leather scraps
Scissors
Fastener tape, such as Velcro
Fabric glue, such as Aleene's Platinum Bond Super Fabric Textile Adhesive
Embroidered butterfly and diamond-shape patches
Star, flower, and round rivets and rivet setter
¼-inch black elastic
Pinking shears
Leather laces
¼-inch ribbon

here's how

1 To make the ponytail wraps, cut the leather into a pair of 3-inch-long strips (3¾ inches for thick hair), the width from 1¼ to 2 inches. Cut the width of the fastener tape in half and trim the length to match the width of your leather strip. Separate the fastener tape. Use fabric glue to attach half of fastener to the underside of each end of the leather strip. Use more fabric glue to attach embroidered patches. Let the glue dry overnight.

2 To make a headband, use an 11-inch length of leather, and cut it 1 to 1¼ inches wide. For the flowered headband, use patterns on *page 75* to cut shapes from leather scraps. To set rivets, use scissors to snip small holes evenly spaced along middle of leather strip and in centers of flower and leaf cutouts. (For help, see Diagrams A–C on *page 75*.) Stack flower shapes and put a set of rivet parts through each hole. Set the back part of the rivet on the rivet base and hammer the pieces together with a rivet setter. Measure a piece of elastic to fit snugly

continued on page 75

Happenin' Hair Accessories

IT'S EASY!

Rivets are those little metal pieces in the center of each flower, right. While they might look tricky to insert, they're really easy! Look on page 75 to see how to set a rivet.

WOVEN RIBBON HEADBAND

FLORAL HEADBAND

FLORAL PONYTAIL WRAP

TASSELED PONYTAIL WRAPS

DIAMOND PONYTAIL WRAP

BUTTERFLY PONYTAIL WRAP

Hair Accessories

continued from page 72

around your head when placed in last rivets on either side of the leather strip. Knot one end through a rivet and then check the length before knotting and cutting the other end.

3 To make the tasseled ponytail wraps, set three star rivets ¼ inch apart down the center of a 3×1¼-inch leather strip. Trim the edges with pinking shears. Make a knot in the center of a 3-inch length of leather lace, fold in half, and

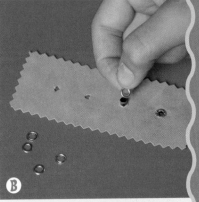

then thread the ends through the rivet; the knot stops it from pulling through. Attach tassels in the rest of the rivets. Add fastener tape as described in Step 1.

4 To make the stitched headband, insert rivets as described in Step 2. Thread ribbon through the flower rivets. Add elastic as described in Step 2.

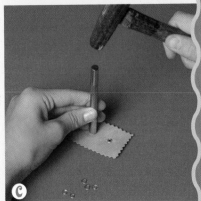

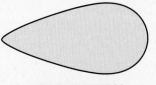

SMALL FLOWER PATTERN

LARGE FLOWER PATTERN

LEAF PATTERN

Nifty Necklaces

what you'll need

Polymer clay, such as Sculpey, in desired colors
Rolling pin; scissors
Decorative-edge scissors
Screwdriver; pencil
Wood skewer
Glass baking dish; cord

here's how

1. Knead a walnut size piece of clay until it is soft and smooth. Roll out clay on a smooth surface until about ⅛ inch thick.

2. Use regular scissors or decorative-edge scissors to cut the clay into the main pendant shape.

3. Decorate the pendant using small pieces of clay. Press balls or other shapes into place and use a screwdriver or pencil point to make more texture.

4. Carefully fold one corner or one side loosely around a wood skewer to make a loop for a cord. Remove the skewer from the clay pendant.

5. Shape clay beads to go on the necklace.

6. Place the clay pieces in a baking dish and ask an adult to bake the clay according to the label on the clay. Let the clay pieces cool.

7. Cut a cord to the length you want to wear it plus 5 inches. String the beads and pendant onto the cord, tie the ends, and trim off the extra cord.

Thread clay
works of art on
a cord to make
rockin' necklaces.

BEADED BARRETTES

Beaded Barrettes and Hair Picks

Make some incredible glass jewelry to wear in your hair! Enjoy making these grown-up style hair picks and barrettes.

what You'll need

Assorted plastic barrettes and hair picks
Double-sided craft tape, such as Terrifically Tacky; glass mosaic beads; micro beads
Clear crafts glue, such as Aleene's Gel Tacky

here's how

1 Cover the plastic back of the barrette or hair pick end with the double-sided tape. Peel off the paper covering and press the mosaic beads onto the sticky tape.

continued on page 80

Beaded Barrette and Hair Picks

continued from page 79

2 Place the barrette or hair pick into a bag of micro beads and move it around until the beads fill all the open spaces on the tape.

3 Arrange and glue beads on micro beads. Let dry. Use a paintbrush to coat micro and larger beads with glue. Let the glue dry before wearing.

BEADED HAIR PICKS

Graffiti Shoes

what You'll need

Fabric shoes
Fabric paints
Paintbrush
Paint pens in colors
    you like
Glitter fabric paint
Gems
Colored ribbon to fit
    shoe eyelets

Your feet want to dance in these fancy, fresh, artist's-style sneakers.

here's how

1 Painting one section at a time, paint the large sections of the shoes using fabric paints and a paintbrush. Paint the edges or shoe trim the colors you like. Let the paint dry.

2 Use paint pens to draw shapes, letters, squiggles, or any other designs you wish on the shoes. Let dry.

3 To put on gems, squeeze a pea-size spot of glitter paint on the shoe and press the gem into the paint. Let it dry.

4 Lace the shoes with colored ribbons.

IT'S EASY!

Have mom buy colored sneakers to save time painting the background. Choose your favorite pair from all the pretty colors and start drawing pretty patterns on your shoes!

Bouquet Brims

Plant all your favorite silk posies on the brim of a visor in minutes!

AMAZING!

Your creative vision will help you design a visor to match every outfit! Use buttons, beads, stickers, old jewelry, and crayons to give personality to a visor brim.

what You'll need

Wire cutters
Silk flowers
Hot-glue gun and glue
  sticks
Plastic visors

here's how

1 Cut the silk flower heads off the stems.

2 Ask an adult to help you hot-glue flowers to the top of visor. If the centers of your flowers come apart, glue them back in place. Let cool.

Fancy purses are "in"-and this
one really grabs the compliments!

Showy Shoulder Bag

what You'll need

Tracing paper; pencil
Scissors
2 felt squares in two
  colors
Fabric tube paints in
  colors similar to felt
3 black buttons
Black perle cotton and
  needle
Thick white crafts glue
8 flat white beads
Make-up style mesh bag
  with zipper
28-inch strip of flat
  braid for strap

here's how

1 Trace patterns, *pages 88–89,* and cut out. Trace around patterns on felt. Cut out flowers from felt. Outline each flower with fabric paint of same color. Let dry.

2 Stack small flowers on top of larger ones. Place a button in the center of each flower.

3 Use a needle threaded with a double strand of perle cotton to sew buttons and flowers to the purse. (See *page 71* for tips on sewing on buttons.) Tie loose ends of perle cotton together on top of buttons to create flower pistils.

4 Tie a knot on each end of the flat braid. Stitch a knot to each side of the purse with a needle and thread.

5 Glue white beads where you wish over the front. Let the glue dry.

continued on page 88

Showy Shoulder Bag

continued from page 87

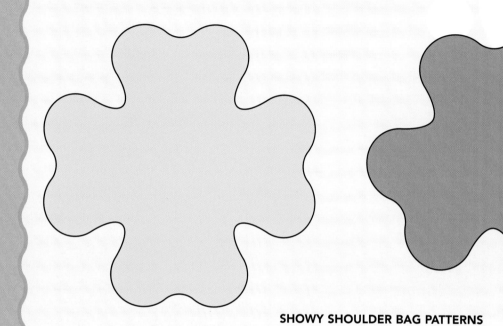

SHOWY SHOULDER BAG PATTERNS

Flowers come in all sorts of shapes. More flower patterns are opposite, and you can also look in your garden for design ideas.

**SHOWY SHOULDER BAG—
ALTERNATE PATTERNS**

89

Potato Beads

what you'll need

Plastic knife
Potato
Wood skewer
Acrylic paints in turquoise and black
Paintbrush
Stippling paintbrush
Silver-tone beads
Leather cord

here's how

1 Use a plastic knife to cut ½- to 1-inch irregular chunks from a potato.

2 Poke a wood skewer into the center of each potato chunk to create a hole for stringing. Leave the potato pieces on the skewer to dry. Drying may take three days to a week. The potato chunks turn black when dry.

3 Leave the potato chunks on the skewer, arranging so there is space between each chunk. Paint the potato pieces turquoise. Let the paint dry.

4 Use a stippling brush to dab small areas of black paint on each turquoise piece. Let the paint dry.

5 Remove the beads from the skewer. Decide the order of the turquoise and silver beads for the necklace and for the bracelet.

6 Cut leather cord for the necklace and bracelet, cutting each piece 5 inches longer than the length you wish. String the beads on the pieces of cord. Knot the ends together for each piece of jewelry.

AMAZING!

Make potato beads look like other stones by simply changing the colors of paint you use. Check out a rock book from the library to get ideas.

No one will guess that your natural turquoise-looking necklace and bracelet are made from potato chunks!

91

4

GO AHEAD–
GET ARTSY!

No Special Reason, Just Craft for the Fun of It

Get your homework out of the way and then make some great stuff like an art caddy, a photo album, and a book cover!

Funky Art Caddy

what You'll need

Clean empty paint can (available in hardware, paint, and home improvement stores)
Acrylic paints, such as Liquitex Glossies, in bright colors
Paintbrush
Strong glue, such as E6000

Paintbrushes, crayons, pencils, or other objects for gluing onto can

Your art supplies will be easy to carry along with this wild and wacky paint pail.

here's how

1 Drip different colors of paint down the edges of the can. Begin with a heavy brush load of paint and wipe it off along the rim of can as if wiping off extra paint from a brush. Paint the center of the lid in the same way. Let the paint dry.

2 Paint each decorative paintbrush handle a solid color; let the paint dry. To paint dots, dip the handle end of another paintbrush into paint and dot onto the surface. To decorate the bristles, dip them in paint

94

Paint stripes or dots on your caddy. To make stripes, use a tiny paintbrush. To make dots, dip a paintbrush handle in paint and dot on the surface. Rinse out the paint from your brush when changing colors.

and let dry. Paint more designs if you wish. Let the paint dry before adding layers.

3 Use strong glue to glue the decorative paintbrushes, crayons, and pencils to the can. Let the glue dry.

4 Fill the can with paintbrushes or other art supplies.

Decorative papers cut with pinking shears and a sprinkling of seed beads wrap a photo album with color and texture.

Patchwork Album

what you'll need

Photo or scrapbook
  album
Acrylic paint in white or
  any color you like
Paintbrush
Decorative papers in
  colors you like
Pinking shears
Decoupage medium
Photo; white paper
Seed beads

here's how

1 If you wish, paint the cover of the photo album with two or three coats of acrylic paint. Let it dry between coats.

2 Use pinking shears to cut pieces of decorative paper into different squares and rectangles.

continued on page 98

Patchwork Album

continued from page 20

Ⓐ Ⓑ

3 Paint decoupage medium onto the album cover front as shown in Photo A. Arrange paper shapes on the decoupage medium as shown in Photo B.

Overlap and paste paper until the background is covered. Coat the papers with decoupage medium as shown in Photo C, *opposite*. Put a photo on the cover.

Brush on a coat of decoupage medium.
4 Trim narrow white paper strips to border the photo. Coat the entire cover with decoupage medium and

sprinkle seed beads onto the wet surface as shown in Photo D. Let dry. Paint two more coats of decoupage medium over the cover, letting dry between coats.

AMAZING!

Put this look on all kinds of things around your room! Decoupage papers and sprinkle beads on flat picture frames, storage boxes, and diary covers.

Locker Hanger

Have all your stuff ready so you can look your best before, during, and after class.

what You'll need

Stiffened felt in three colors
Scissors
Pencil
Letter template (stencil)
Strong glue, such as E6000; plate
Decorative-edge scissors
Glass paints in bottles with fine tip for painting
Comb; brush
Mirror (small enough to fit inside your locker door)
Adhesive hook-and-loop tape, such as Velcro
Magnetic strips

here's how

1 Cut a rectangular piece of felt to fit inside your locker door.

2 Use a letter template to trace the letters of your name on felt. Cut out the letters.

3 Cut a rectangular piece of felt large enough to fit the letters.

4 Cut a shape larger than the mirror from another piece of felt. Use a plate or any round object to trace the shape if the mirror is round. Use strong adhesive to glue it onto rectangle.

5 Cut a strip of felt to go on the bottom using decorative-edge scissors.

6 Use glass paints in tubes with fine tips for painting to decorate a brush, comb, and mirror.

7 Use strong glue to attach the mirror to the felt.

8 Attach adhesive hook-and-loop tape to the backs of the brush and comb.

9 Place other side of hook-and-loop tape (Velcro) onto the felt.

10 Cut small magnetic strips and use strong glue to glue them on the back of the felt. Let dry before using.

IT'S EASY!

Make an organizer like this one for your bedroom! Instead of hanging it in a locker, make it to fit the back of your bedroom or closet door.

Just the right size to hold your ballet slippers and a leotard or two, this adorable bag has painted shoes with real ribbon ties.

Tu-Tu Cute Ballet Bag

what You'll need

Tracing paper
Pencil
Scissors
Fabric tote bag
Acrylic enamel paint,
    such as Liquitex
    Glossies, in pink or
    other color you like
Paintbrush
Thick white crafts glue
Glitter
½- and ⅛-inch satin
    ribbons
Strong glue, such
    as E6000
Sequins on a string

here's how

1 Trace the ballet shoes pattern on *page 104* or the tap shoe pattern on *page 105* onto tracing paper. Cut out and trace onto bag.

2 Paint the shoes pink or any color of acrylic enamel paint you like. Let the paint dry.

3 To add glitter on the shoes, paint on a thin coat of crafts glue where you want sparkle. Sprinkle on glitter. Let dry.

4 Cut ½-inch-wide ribbon to make the shoe ties. Glue in place with a dot of strong glue.

5 Use strong glue to hold sequin trim along the edges of the bag and the open area of the shoe design. Let the glue dry.

6 Wrap the handles with narrow ribbon and glue in place. Tie ribbon bows at the bottom of each handle.

continued on page 104

AMAZING!

Whatever your hobby, make a tote that shows your interest! Just imagine the clever designs for your tote...musical notes, postage stamps, soccer ball, ice skates, your favorite animals...the possibilities are endless!

Tu-Tu Cute Ballet Bag

continued from page 103

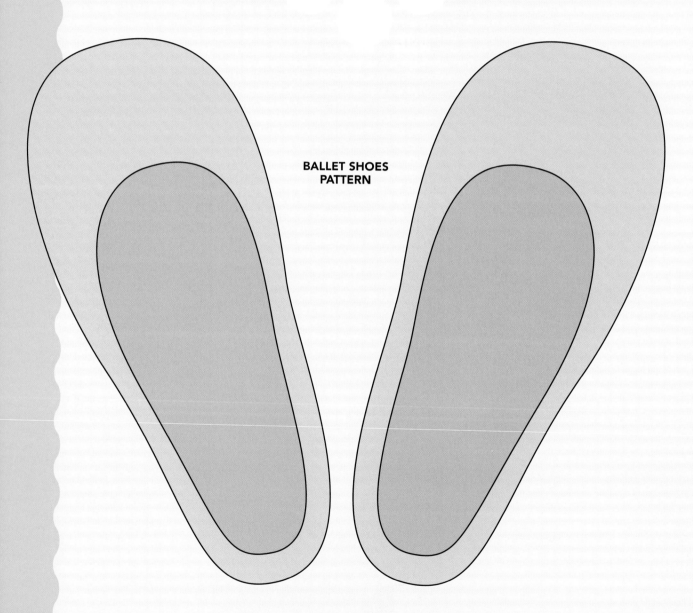

BALLET SHOES PATTERN

ALTERNATE BALLET BAG PATTERN—TAP SHOE

Trim egg shapes with clay details to make little characters to brighten your room.

what You'll need

Air-dry clay, such as Crayola Model Magic
Plaster or wood eggs
Dull knife
Feather
Pencil
Thick white crafts glue
Acrylic paints in pink, lavender, yellow, green, blue, gray, and orange

here's how

1 Make clay feet for the creatures that have feet. To make pig feet, roll four balls the size of large grapes and shape them into cylinders. To make bunny feet, roll two balls and press in on one side. To make bird feet, use two grape-size balls, shape into a diamond shape, and press in on one side. Shape critter hands with your fingers. Use a dull knife to make creases on feet, hands, and fins.

2 Shape fish fins and pig ears by rolling out dough to ⅛-inch thickness. Cut out fin or ear shapes. To make a bird nose, shape a small triangle. Make a small cone shape for the top of the bird head and pierce a hole in it for the feather. To make a pig nose, roll a small grape-size ball and flatten it against the end of the egg. Make nostrils using a pencil point. To

continued on page 108

Crazy Critters

Crazy Critters

continued from page 107

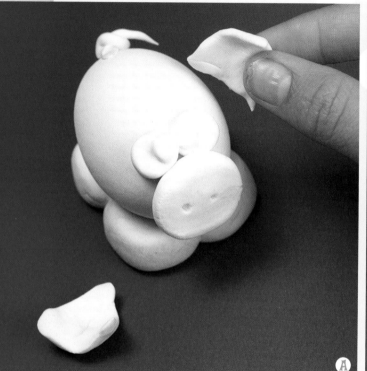

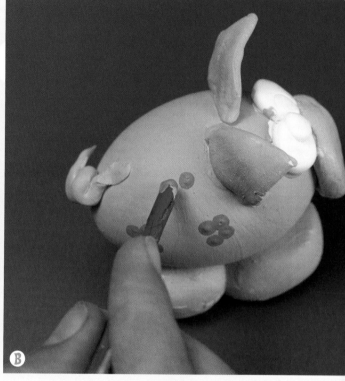

A **B**

make whites of eyes, form round raisin-size balls and flatten onto face. Make smaller balls for the colored portions of eyes. Press onto whites. Glue pieces on the eggs as shown in Photo A. Let dry.

3 Paint the base colors, painting the critter around eyes. Let dry.

4 To paint eyes, make dots by dipping the handle of a small paintbrush into paint and dotting onto the egg.

Paint flowers, stripes, checks, or any pattern you wish on the egg critters as shown in Photo B. Let the paint dry.

5 Glue a feather into the hole in the top of the bird head.

IT'S EASY!

Once you see how easy these critters are to make, continue creating other favorite animals. Just look at a picture and shape the clay pieces to match. Before you know it, you'll have enough to fill a miniature zoo!

smarty-pants pillows

what you'll need

Pants or overalls
Pillow form, 12×16 or
    14×14 inches; scissors
White thread
Sewing machine
Crafting foam scraps
Paper punch
Paint marker
Bead and glass glue,
    such as Aleene's
    Platinum Bond
Rhinestones
1½-inch sheer ribbon
½-inch cotton trim

When you outgrow your favorite pants, transform them into decorative pillows to toss on your bed!

here's how

1 Place the pillow form over the pants, lining up the waist with the top of the pillow. Have an adult

continued on page 112

Smarty-Pants Pillows

continued from page 111

help you cut off the bottom of the pants 2 inches below the bottom of the pillow form. Cut apart the seam on the inside of the pant legs.

2 Working on the wrong side of the pants, pin the cut seams together at the center front and center back of the pants. Ask an adult to help you machine-stitch a straight seam down from the zipper at the front and another straight seam down from the seat at the back. Turn the pants right side out to check whether the fabric lays flat. Sew the bottom edges of the pants together. Place the pillow form inside the pants and then stitch the waist closed.

3 For the overalls pillow, stitch the bottom of the overall front to the bottom edge of the front of the pillow and then stitch the back of the overalls to the bottom edge of the back of the pillow.

4 To finish either pillow, cut a shape out of the crafting foam and punch a hole in one end.

Write something on the foam piece with paint marker. Use glue to glue a rhinestone to the decorated tag. Thread the cotton trim through the hole and then thread it through a belt loop or wrap it around an overall strap. Tie the ends in a bow. Thread sheer ribbon through belt loop or around a pillow detail and tie into a bow.

AMAZING!

Use your pillow for a friendship symbol. The next time the girls are over, let them sign their names on the front using paint pens or permanent marking pens.

what you'll need

Suitcase; masking tape
Newspapers; white spray
primer, such as KILZ
Hot pink spray paint
Silk flowers; wire cutter
Hot-glue gun; glue sticks

here's how

1 Begin with a clean, dry suitcase. Put masking tape over any areas you do not want painted, such as the hardware.

2 In a well-ventilated work area, cover the surface with newspapers.

Have an adult help spray-paint the suitcase with a light coat of primer. Let it dry. Spray on a second coat; let dry.

3 Spray on two light coats of hot pink paint, letting the paint dry between coats.

4 Cut the flower heads off of the stems.

5 Ask a grown-up to help you hot-glue flowers on the case top. If the flower centers come apart, reglue them. Glue a flower on each side of the case.

Girls go ga ga over this overnight case!

Think Pink Suitcase

When magazine pages make you smile, use them to design a cool carryall and share the fun with everyone!

She's Got Rhythm

Personality Purses

what You'll need

Magazines to cut up
Scissors or paper cutter
Newspapers
Spray adhesive
Clear adhesive paper,
  such as Con-Tact
Sewing machine; thread
Paper punch
Eyelets and eyelet tool
Beaded string, cord,
  chain, or other trim
Ball chain connector,
  optional

here's how

1 Find pictures and words you like in magazines. Remove the pages.

2 From magazine pages, cut out four large purse sides (however big you want the purse), two for the outside and two to line the inside.

3 For the narrow ends, cut four 2½-inch-wide strips that are the same height as purse. For the bottom, cut two 2½-inch-wide strips the same width as the purse.

4 In a well-ventilated work area, cover the surface with newspapers. Have an adult spray adhesive on the back of each magazine piece; press onto lining.

5 Cover both sides of each piece with clear self-adhesive paper, trimming at page edges.

6 Ask an adult to help you machine-sew the purse sides to the narrow end strips using a zigzag stitch. Sew the bottom to the purse. Zigzag-stitch around the purse top.

7 To make holes for the handle, punch a hole in the center of each side strip about ½ inch from the top. Use the eyelet tool to secure eyelets.

8 Cut 2 yards of beaded string for a double handle or 1 yard for a single. Insert it through both eyelets. Secure the ends together with a ball chain connector or knot. If using cord or other trim, pull through and knot.

what you'll need

Felts in colors you like
Book to be covered
Ruler
Marking pen
Scissors
Thick white crafts glue
Masking tape
Decorative-edge
  scissors
Sequins or gems,
  optional

here's how

1 Lay felt on a smooth work surface. Lay the book down, opened and centered on top of the felt. Use a marking pen to draw a line 2 inches from the top of the book and 2 inches from the bottom. Measure the width of the book cover and use that measurement minus 2 inches to draw the lines on the sides as shown in Photo A. Cut the felt along the edge of the book binding. Cut out the felt.

2 With book laying open, fold the top panel inward and glue the wide panel onto it as shown in Photo B. Tape in place with masking tape until glue dries. Glue the other panel in place the same way.

3 Cut out a cover design from felt. Use decorative-edge scissors to cut strips of felt or any simple shape you want. Glue the shapes on the cover. Trim with sequins or gems if you wish.

Bold Book Covers

Cover an extra special book
with felt in all your
favorite colors and shapes.

Doodled Surprise

Make a good friend's day with a jigsaw puzzle that's a blast to put together.

what You'll need

Pencil
Blank jigsaw puzzle
  (available in crafts and
  art stores)
Permanent marking
  pens in black and
  desired colors
Adhesive gems
Stickers

here's how

1 Using a pencil, draw words and pictures on the puzzle. When you like the design, draw over it with a black marking pen.

2 Use the marking pens to color in the drawing. Draw other details on the puzzle using the black marking pen.

3 Press gems and stickers on the puzzle, making sure they do not go beyond the edge of the puzzle piece.

In-the-Swim Beach Pail

This bright beach pail carries your gear to the shore and then holds found treasures to carry back home.

what you'll need

Pail
Acrylic paints in yellow,
  white, red, and blue
Paintbrush; pencil
Tracing paper; scissors
Jumbo rickrack

here's how

1 Paint the background areas of the pail, painting a yellow stripe on the top and bottom with white in between. Let dry.

2 Trace the patterns, *below*. Cut out. Trace around the shapes on the pail using the photo, *opposite*, as a guide. For the zigzag, trace the edges of a piece of jumbo rickrack. Paint the fish yellow and the bubbles blue. Let dry. Add white highlights on bubbles and red details on fish; let dry.

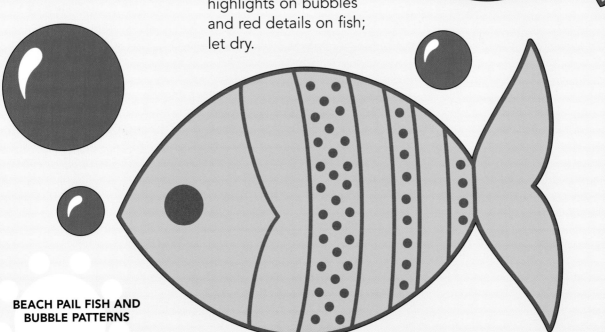

BEACH PAIL FISH AND
BUBBLE PATTERNS

Glossary

Acrylic Paint—water-based paint that dries quickly and cleans up with soap and water. Some are made for outdoor use while others are for inside use only.

Ball Chain Connector—a small metal tube made to hold two ends of a ball chain together.

Base Color/Coat—a first coat of paint that is used to prepare a surface for more paint or to provide a background color.

Decoupage—the technique of cutting out designs (usually from paper) and putting them on a surface using decoupage medium or a half-and-half mixture of glue and water.

Dressmaker's Pencil—a pencil made to write on fabric.

Enamel Paint—a glossy, solid-color paint used to decorate a variety of surfaces. Enamel paint can be water- or oil-based.

Fringe—a border or trim of cords or threads hanging loose or tied in bunches.

Gems—in crafting terms, a plastic rhinestone or smooth colorful stone that is backed with metallic silver to make it sparkle.

Glass Paint—a water-based, shiny paint created to paint on glass surfaces. Some of these paints require oven-baking after an object is painted.

Glossy—having a smooth, shiny appearance or finish.

Grosgrain Ribbon—a flat (not shiny) ribbon with a thin striped texture.

Inseam—the length of pants from the bottom leg to the center seam.

Knead—to mix by pressing and squeezing materials, such as clay, together.

Letter Template—an alphabet stencil made from heavy paper or plastic to use in lettering.

Mosaic Beads—tiny round bead-like embellishments to be glued on a surface, not sewn or strung.

Pipe Cleaner—a velvety covered wire (chenille stem) that can be purchased in a variety of sizes and colors, including metallic. Some pipe cleaners are striped.

Rickrack—found in fabric stores, this is a wavy trim that comes in many sizes, patterns, and colors.

Rivet—a metal tube-like item available in circles and other shapes that is crimped with a tool to attach it. Rivets are used to attach items together or to leave a finished-looking hole.

Seed Beads—tiny round glass beads.

Shank Button—a button with a metal loop on the back that holds the thread.

Stippling Paintbrush—a brush with lots of short, hard bristles used to dab paint through a stencil.

Technique—the method used to do artwork, such as beading, painting, or decoupaging.

Texture—the appearance or feel of a surface.

Tracing—drawing around an object or copying the lines of drawn art.

Tracing Paper—a thin sheet of see-through paper used to trace drawings or patterns.

Vellum—a cloudy paper available in white and colors.

Wrong Side—the side that lacks a design or finish.

Sources

Beads

Gay Bowles Sales/Mill Hill
P.O. Box 1060
Janesville, WI 53547
www.millhill.com
800-356-9438

Westrim Trimming
Corporation
9667 Cantoga Ave.
Chatsworth, CA 91331
www.westrimcrafts.com
818-998-8550

Buttons

JHB International
1955 S. Quince St.
Denver, CO 80231
303-751-8100

Clay

Polyform Products Co.
1901 Estes Ave.
Elk Grove Village, IL 60007
www.sculpey.com

Crayola Model Magic
www.crayola.com
800-CRAYOLA

Decorative-Edge Scissors

Fiskars Consumer Products
305 84th Ave. S.
Wausau, WI 54401
www.fiskars.com
715-842-2091

Decoupage Medium

Plaid Enterprises
P.O. Box 2835
Norcross, GA 30091
800-842-4197

Embroidery Floss

Anchor Consumer Service
P.O. Box 27067
Greenville, SC 29616

DMC
Port Kearney Bldg. 10
South Kearney, NJ 07032

Glass Paint

Delta Tech. Coatings, Inc.
2550 Pellissier Pl.
Whittier, CA 90601
800-423-4135

Liquitex Glossies
Binney & Smith, Inc.
Easton, PA 18044

Paint

Plaid Enterprises
P.O. Box 2835
Norcross, GA 30091
800-842-4197

DecoArt Paint
P.O. Box 386
Stanford KY 40484
800-367-3047

Ribbon

C. M. Offray & Son, Inc.
Rt. 24, Box 601
Chester, NJ 07930
908-879-4700

Thick White Crafts Glue

Aleene's Tacky Glue
www.duncancrafts.com

Wire

Artistic Wire, Ltd.
P.O. Box 1347
Elmhurst, IL 60126
www.artisticwire.com
630-530-7567

Twisteez
www.twisteez.com

Index

If you like this book, try these other crafts books for kids

Credits

Models

Hanna Allison
...mes
...lume
...Bramow
...ey Carlson
...unningham
...a DeJong
...n Gray
...atsuyama
...Matsuyama
...Moore
...n Petterson
...nzie Robbins
...Schoulte
...nith
...a Tusa
...Wetzel

Styling Assistant
...hesnut

...ers
...ker
...oyd
...unstan
...etzel
...Vetzel
...Vetzel

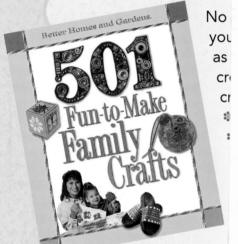

No...
you...
as...
cr...
cr...

W...
w...
...